MOOD SWINGS

POEMS and OTHER RANTS

SECOND EDITION

URIAH BELL

RISING VOICES PRESS
YOUR VOICE AFFIRMED

Mood Swings: poems and other rants
Copyright © 2011 by Uriah Bell

Published by:

Rising Voices Press
P. O. Box 230823
Boston, MA 02123

All rights reserved. No part of this book may be reproduced, performed, recorded, copied, stored in a retrieval system or otherwise transmitted in any form or by any means without permission in writing from the author and publisher, except in the case of reviews. All inquiries must be addressed to Rising Voices Press.

ISBN – 10: 0-615-51553-X
ISBN – 13: 978-0-615-51553-3
Library of Congress Control Number: 2011912778

This book is dedicated to the memory of my grandmother, Mary Ann Bell. Thank you for being my biggest fan, my biggest supporter, and the only constant thing in my life. You encouraged me to dream big, gave me permission to stumble and fall, and believed that I never made a wrong decision no matter how unconventional it was.

MOOD SWINGS

POEMS and OTHER RANTS

SECOND EDITION

RISING VOICES PRESS
YOUR VOICE AFFIRMED

MOOD SWINGS

This is me in black and white
And still filled with color,
Figuratively abstract, and
As apparent as each day.

I'm simply complex, and
As predictable as the weather,
A turbulent wave brushing
Upon the sands serene landscape.

I'm everything and nothing,
Timeless and trendy,
depending on the mood
An outgoing introvert with no cares.

I can be callous and caring,
Couth and cruel,
Predictably unexpected
With stiffening stares.

I'm a pendulum of emotions
A new vibe with each swing
Embrace Newton's cradle –
Figure out the science if you can.

I'm a book open to the public,
A song for the world to sing,
A cement-covered teardrop –
Hiding myself from everything.

ALPHABET SOUP

Antonio.

Brian.

Carlos. Christian.

Damon.

De Andre.

Eliazer.

Elliot and Eric.

Frank.

George. Greg. Gio.

Hector.

Ismael.

Javier. Juan. Jose. (my Latin phase)

Kevin. Keon.

Larry.

Mike(s). Marty.

Nelson.

Noel.

Octavious.

Paul.

Quartez (such a Black name)

Rickey. Ryan. Robert.

Sean. Shannon. Shawn.

Tony. Terrance (Tre for short)

Ulrich.

Valentino.

William.

Xavier.

Yusef.

Zachary.

SLUT.

PET PEEVES

Being on time has
Become a habit of mine, and
I just loathe the queens
Who prance into the functions
With their boosted Bottega bags,
Flossing like they copped it – legit.

And what about the ones
Who dare
Stick their noses in the air
Because of a bit of good fortune
They lucked up on?
Truth be told, the best money is old and
As easy as it comes it's gone.

I hate top boys who bend,
And high pitched, limp wrists
Ball girls that want to climb your back.

I frown at self-limitations
And nervous hesitations
To get out of life what
It is you want; yet you'll
Come to me with the expectation
That what's mine is equally yours.
Failure to plan doesn't mean
Life dealt you a shitty hand, and
NO, what's mine is not ours.

I'm over the boys that

Treat hearts like toys

And emotions like a game of checkers.

They make you fall hard

Letting down your guard

Leaving you with feelings of emptiness.

PRIVATE PARTS

You reached into my shorts and
Touched my private parts.
Your warmth
Made me react, and so with
Every stroke, I throbbed to a different beat.
I closed
My eyes and gave you control.
Your tongue
Traced my abs, goatee sweeping the moisture,
Yours and mine.
My nipples and my dick stood
Firm and strong.

You parted my thighs, assuming permission
To enter. Locking your tongue with mine,
You were,
IN, with one easy stroke.
My back arched before I was on my side
You reached new depths with every thrust.
Knees to my chest, I've never felt you or
Anyone like this.
The sheets glued to me, by my release
I felt you explode inside –
This was *love*
We lay together until the sunrise,
I opened my eyes to witness a shadow of
You,

Creeping out the door, I knew you were
No more.

You reached into my mind and touched
My private parts.

FORGOTTEN

I've lost your embrace

Your kisses, your touch.

You're a stranger to me

Lying idly,

Beside me

Nightly.

I have no idea where the fire's gone.

My former exhibitionist, now

Lazy and listless

When it comes to me.

WHEN A STRANGER CALLS

When a stranger calls,
I am hesitant to answer.
You're an image, the perfect prose
On my IM screen.

Your rhetoric stimulates me, but
Our conversations are not of a
Sexual nature.
My curiosity, not my penis is erect.

Don't get me wrong, when this
Stranger calls, my lips and my… sex
Moistens, as if he has just
Raised my right leg to his left shoulder
In preparation for his entrance.
But, I've gotten of course.

This dark mysterious stranger, whose
Eyes tell his story, and whose
Smile encompasses my soul has
Given me the unimaginable.
He's given me the strength, courage and
More importantly, the desire
To love again.

BACK BURNER – FINALLY A POEM FOR ME

He's worn societies burdens,
From his first sunrise,
And pain has been the only
Consistent thing in his life.
Yet tried and true,
He pushes through,
Anticipating fates next move.

Pain and rejection echo in his head, while
Emptiness partners with him in his bed.
That secret shelf of his,
Where only his burdens lay,
Is becoming weak,
And beginning to bow.

Ask him how he does it,
he'll swear it's the only way he
knows.
He's allowed many to enter,
But few have remained,
All exiting with a pitiable reason.
No formidable opponent in
This game of life and love
All eliminated due to treason.

His burner is hot with desolation

Fueling his fire,

A sign on his heart reads,

"compassion for hire".

Each day a new trial for him to bear,

With no one to love and so much love to share.

A POEM FORGOTTEN ...

Boomerang me baby, just toss me
And I'll come back.
I'll be back, but not with any
notice.
You see, I'll hide away and
Come back with a piercing blow,
Making you regret your actions.
Toss me, toss me hard, and the
Wind will carry me in a long
Ovular motion, blowing harder in my return baby,
Cause
You see, I've been boomeranged before, so
It's nothing new.
Just boomerang me baby, and oh yeah
Oh yeah,
I'll come back to you.

LIAR LIAR

We've come upon a celebration
Of years in each others' lives, but
It seems that celebration
Was only one of festering lies.

It's like I'm involved with *two* people
You act one way in, and another out,
But I've asked around, and people tell me
That's not what love's about.

It seems we've lost, or never had
What any relationship needs as ground,
And I write these words with mixed emotions
Not knowing what's to come in the next round.

Bygones are supposed to be bygones, but
That's much easier said than done,
This last bout with doubt hit me hard
And I think you've played all your cards.

You have nothing to hang over my head
We promised the last time would be the end
But the cat was away, and the mouse tried to play
And my lover's no longer my friend, and
Any love without trust as its base is as
Secure as a house build on sand.

I'm so hesitant to see where

The next round takes us

When all I wanted and needed was for us to go higher,

My heart can't ignore all the things you've done,

My dear liar liar.

VACATION

Pain has invaded my heart

That private spot where

Your love once dwelled.

Thirty-two short days of contentment

Paraded to a halt by deceit-

I'm not surprised.

I gave you entrance where

No one should, the ultimate

Permission to destroy me;

I set myself up for disappointment

And betrayal.

I hope you're happy.

Why

Am

I

Not

Surprised?

ALONG FOR THE RIDE

I've given you too much too soon
You're taking my love
My time, and my life for granted.
Eyes wide shut, I'm here, alone
Along for the ride.

You're slipping into the ordinary, a
Like the rest of them kind of man.
Becoming everything you said you wouldn't be,
And now I sit here, idly, uncontrollably
Helplessly along for the ride,
Alone, for this ride of love.

OVERDOSE

If what they say is true, that
The best things in life are free,
Then why is it that I'd pay
A mint for you?

I'd get my dimes
And pennies together
Rob from the rich
To give one assuring
Night with you.
I'd write a bad check and
Watch it bounce for days
In my afterglow.

Eyes red from smoking the herbs of ecstasy
With you sayin'
"I'm your pusher man, inhale to a new high".

Ooh, can you feel it?
Can you feel the slammin' grooves of our night,
Last night?
I awaken from my high
Not a dime to my name and debts to pay.
You were my pusher man
My lover.
I exhaled and died.

A POEM FOR DENNIS

if I lay down and die tonight
would you cry for me in the mornin'
would you smile as I entered heaven,
as delicate cherubs blew their horns?

would you have a service in my honor
reciting feelings I never knew,
would you sing a song of heavenly praise
as I smiled down upon you?

would you be happy just to know
that my soul was finally at ease,
would you smile as you stroll the park
knowing I was the rustle in the autumn leaves?

and as you look into the midnight sky
there's one thing I'd ask you to do,
find the brightest star amongst the heavens, and
know that it's me watching over you.

as you sit outside in the spring, and
see a butterfly spread it's wings
that'll be me saying hello, and
just know that it was my time to go.

would you pack away and save
all the lovely treasures I gave?
would you dance to my favorite song
as the melody lingered on?

would you visit me every now and then
staying as strong as a thousand men,
would you still notice a cardinals call, or
would you remember me at all?

the most important of all these things –
when an eagle spreads its' wings
as rare as it seems to be…
know that I am finally free.

FALLING APART

I cry solid

harsh tears;

heavy puddles of

black tears

carrying memories

of how life

used

to

be.

Not memories of beaten and battered blues,

but of the ease and comfort of life.

I cry black tears

thick crude oil tears;

rich and priceless

memories I savor.

The oil falls onto my tongue

swallowing it's many delights

enticing my palate.

My stomach turns

like tears / memories

turn sour.

I feel sick,

violently ill, and now

my candy coated rich oil tears

like life

has turned on me

causing internal anguish.

JUST A THOUGHT

I've forgotten how to write a poem
>> OR

is it

that I have nothing to write about

except

AIDS

having no car in the winter

withering love

infidelity

fears

job security

education
>> TIME.

Sins.

Nah, there's nothing to write about,

but,

sickness
>> fatigue

that sexy ass boy in gate F3

dysfunctional family life,

a drunken pilot,

wanting to be free from it all

but living off everyday stress;

the woman coughing her airborne… next to me

the white boy with the big piece in the plaid pajama pants with the Oklahoma accent -
wanting more from a friend than any friend should give.

Dammit, can someone refresh me on how to do this poem thing?

DROWNING

When I lay down at night
I wonder.
I wonder if my stress will
allow me to open my tear filled
eyes in the morning, or
will my stress, with its overwhelming
abundance pull me below
deep into my abyss, where I will
lose my breath in my involuntary
gasps of air?

In my tossing and turning, my
eyes unfold, and I see space.
Empty
troublesome space, and I prepare
to enter a nonchalant and uncaring society
ready to burden me with affliction.

THROUGH MY EYES

Look at our love through my eyes, and
you'll see the future is dim.
We're from two different worlds, with
beliefs and backgrounds
that we can't compromise, you'll see,
if you look through my eyes.

You'll see,
communication gaps, and
oh how you snap,
issues within;
here we go again,
with – I need to
straighten up my act, no
opposites don't attract.
You'll see through the lies,
if you look through my eyes.

BOTTOMS UP

There's a forbidden excitement
about the men who are
man enough to receive another.

They possess a power that
allows them to love, and to
be hurt repeatedly,
simultaneously;
a power that makes them real.
To receive and never deliver, to display
their incomparable agility.

When a man has such remarkable control
over his body and yours.
Bottoms up to my bottoms,
those who dance and get *us* sprung.
the men with that natural sway
in their hips, and unrelenting
venom in their lips.

A man that can ride you, feigning submission
yet never relinquishing control.
A man's man.
A real man.

This one's for my bottoms.

LESSON IN LOVE

Stop, look, listen

To my heart, and

You'll hear it beat

Echoing cries for our love.

Listen, without

Cutting me off, and

You'll know that

I want nothing but life's

Best for you.

Look into my eyes

To see the things

My head won't let my

Heart reveal.

Take this time to

Love me, and

To let me love you,

No restrictions

No limitations.

Speak to me

Not with defense in your voice, but

With the tone of love.

Cry with me

Let me know that

You too are real.

Stop refusing me

Accept me

As only I can be.

Look at how far we've come
Don't let society or the church
Take that away.
Listen to your heart – for once.
It's time to live.
For you.

WORK IN PROGRESS . . . A POEM FOR BRIAN

he lives his life for others, expecting nothing

more than what's thrown his way;

burdened with confliction of his own identity -

he's alone

consumed with a battlefield of heart

his own internal purgatory

will he abandon all he's known

for a half and twenty – three years, or

will he follow his heart – this time?

will he acknowledge and accept this love

so taboo, so forbidden, so true?

he is a work in progress

learning to accept himself

while showing others the way.

YESTERDAY

Your generic tone beguiles me -
I struggle to know what it is you feel
Do you love me like your boy, or do you love me like your man?
Am I your forever throughout and through in true love, or
am I merely your friend?

Are you wasting your time with me, and
more importantly, am I wasting mine?
Am I a filler task in your present agenda, and
would it be easier if I surrender?

Tell me the truth,
stop shielding me with lies,
what you've put me through has made me stronger
able to rise above this flood of cries.

Shame on you for using me
like an ever-flowing resource in your life,
shame on me for giving you the power
to cause this anguish and strife.

My emotions are running empty
My heart's growing numb
My energy level is depleting
My desire has gone
My heart knows better
My mind agrees

It's time to be selfish, and
do what's best for me.

Today is the beginning
yesterday has gone
tomorrow composes new lyrics
in my life's song,
so in a four-fourth tempo
I must say goodbye
to a love I thought was true
and face the realization
that you're simply someone I once knew.

NO RESERVATIONS

Other brothas have phoned ahead
and stepped up in this establishment
not in proper dress code, but you;
you need no reservations
you have all access.
Dine in or carry out kind of love
start a tab, no credit checks needed.

I'll give you extra helpings
with free sides
keep you full
satisfy your cravings,
I'll save the seat by the window
and near the fireplace
making sure you're warm while inside.

Don't worry 'bout being greedy
cause my love flows freely
when you need some lovin'
have no hesitations
come on inside
with no reservations

SIGNING OFF

I've stayed on for too long,
my time on air has gone,
I've given you all of me, and you give
of yourself in rations
I fight for your time, attention and passion.

I know you're ashamed of who you are,
and what's worse is you're ashamed of me,
my persistence and love for you brings me back, but
in my heart I know this is no place to be.

To wake up in the morning telling myself
this is the day,
wanting so much to love you
but needing even more to pull away.

The pleasure in my heart is gone
hurt has found its place there,
The thought of losing you was always my fear,
and now I can't say that I care.

I'm signing off from this situation
one that I never should've gotten into,
you shouldn't take it personal, but
then again emotions aren't you.

It's time to look out for me
you've been first far too long
walking away won't be easy
but, I know you'll be strong.

Go back to your old ways
and, I'll finally work on me,
maybe we'll meet in our tomorrows
if it's truly meant to be.

But as for today,
I have to say goodbye
I'm signing off of what began as love
but reared its ugly head a lie.

THE DETACHED

When I
Lay in your arms
I'm seeking shelter.
The beat
of your heart
stabs me in
my back.
Your words carve
and your
breath on my necks nape
cut through me
to the bone like the
bitter New England winter.
Your hollow embrace
is
suffocating,
an evaporating mist of nothingness –
taking my life with it.

HINDSIGHT

If I could, I'd tell you how selfish you were
For not being there for me
The way I was there for you.

If I could, I'd take back my time, my energy
And all I've given up for you.

If I could, I'd kick my own ass for being your fool,
And your ass for lying to me, for making me your marionette
A simple hobby to satisfy your deepest pleasures and curiosities.

If I could, I'd spill your tea, putting it all out there
Only so you'll know the hurt you've introduced to me.

If I could, I'd force your feet in my shoes.
You wouldn't be able to take a step,
Less walk a mile in my life.

If I had the chance I'd tell you
How weak you really are.

If I could, I'd tell you how cold your touch, and
Hollow your voice is.
I'd remind you how much you'd miss me
When you awake tomorrow and find me gone.

If I knew how, I'd prepare you for
The extinction of what was never there,
The cold of what's dead would chill you, but
Your arrogance would surely keep you warm.

If you felt my pain, or cried my tears
You'd emerge from your lonely world
And wrap your arms around me locking me
In the embrace I'd been longing for.

If I could, I'd leave without saying goodbye
Without a care of how you'd go on, but assured
I'd make it without you.

If I could, I'd tell you how much I hate you
How much I love you, I'd tell you the truth.

RENEGE

you said our love was unconditional
communication flowed freely, but
you took it back

your embrace protected me
your words helped me through the day, but
you took them back

you spoke of visions of the future
but you took them back

I gave you all of me, but
you gave it back.

UNCONVENTIONAL ME

you won't find me
in the same old place
doing the same old things
with the same old folks

not feelin' the bars
the clubs, no room
for online *love*

give me contemporary art
the symphony, midnight walks along the beach
solo, of course
I'm into me time
meaning without you

give me my tenor sax
some cognac
the first lady of song with
a full moon shining, or a crackling fire

I like to walk around free
rediscover me
learn my ins and outs
and what I'm all about

layin' in the tub
showing myself some love
moanin' and groanin' and
I do it all alone

and for the first time in my life
I'm okay with loving me
unconditionally
unconventionally
me

BITTER

I've heard that line of yours
A time or two about
How you feel bad
That I didn't get to cum.

But you explode your
Weak ass load at the
First roll of my tongue.

I lay there waiting for
Some reciprocation, and
Repeatedly there's none.

I never lied about
Getting mine on the side
And now you come to me
So desperately talkin'
About those bitch ass nights
When you cried.

Now you look at me
With crazy eyes
When I tell you
All we can be is boys, but
Your pride won't
Allow you to apologize
To this heart
Your selfishness destroyed.

NUMB

Hatred can be justified by this coldness in my heart
and every past tear measured,
Fear of loneliness can be explained by former loves lost
and memories good and bad treasured.

This yearning I feel to simply be alone
the *books* classify as a guise,
It's in the company of solitude, and only there
that no one can hear my cries.

The joy I see, if only in my dreams
is enough to fill me up on hope,
but it's with the nightmares of my reality
that I find it impossible to cope.

The numbness that consumes me,
is a feeling all to familiar,
to not hate, nor love, nor care nor want
is anything but peculiar.

LOCK THE DOOR

(a barber's tale)

for six years we've had a standing *appointment*
every Saturday at two,
a shop always filled with clients
our words always few.

empty talks about music and sports
your women of course,
all the while lining my face
with gentle force.

you licked your lips
while studying my face
the air thick with pseudo masculinity
I was always out of place.

last week was different somehow,
I couldn't figure out why,
the shop was empty
only you and I.

your tone was different
your questions probing
by the end of my cut
my thickness was throbbing.

six years of suppression
couldn't be ignored
as I stood to reach for you
you said '*lock the door*'.

I stepped to you
your ass cupped by my hand
I pulled you close, showing you
what makes a man a man.

I invited you into my mouth
using my tongue as your guide
then you displayed your agility
as I made my way inside.

you insisted
you've never done this before
I promised
you'd come back for more.

we were at all angles
on the counters, across the chair
you screamed you couldn't take it
and whispered you didn't care.

before I knew it
you were begging for more
I said 'but baby'
you moaned 'fuck what I said before'.

at your direction I pounded deeper
you handled it like a pro
I decided to tease it, and
take it nice and slow

that rhythm drove you mad
with the longest and deepest of thrusts
then you started shaking and hissed
SHIT – I'm about to bust!

I felt you tighten from the inside
as you generously released your load
and without warning, your clenching tightness
made me explode.

the ecstasy of a fire ignited
was a power we couldn't ignore
but it came to an end abruptly – aw shit
we didn't lock the door.

LOVE AND PAIN

the route that our hearts travel

cannot be guided by positioning systems

or directional references

there are no road signs

and U turns are not allowed

our hearts navigate on experience

using past hurts and past loves

as reference points and landmarks

for those brave enough to dare out

on the road of love

there are only two rewards in the end-

love and pain.

INSEPARABLE

You are my midnight sky
Dark and calming as such
I embrace you as we make love
I am your moon, look into my light, but
Don't let my love overwhelm you into
Uncontrollable rolling waves of aggression.

I am your tree, you are my soil
Nourish me love, in turn
I'll give you oxygen and energy.
We can produce. *Re* produce.
Together. Forever. Me. You.

You are my butterfly
Beautiful and unique
Me, your leaf.
Consume me in my entirety.
Gone
All gone, but
Always more.

You are my sun, but I'm the shine.
You are my poem, but I'm the rhyme.
You're my gift, and I'm the wrap.
You're my destination and I'm the map.
You're the sheets and I'm the bed.
I'm all the thoughts that fill your head.

You're my angel, and I'm your wings.
I'm the song that you're to sing.
You're my door, but I'm the key,
Without you, there is no me.
You're the apple of my eye,
We're inseparable, you and I.

NIGHT

At night when I step into the bath,
I close my eyes and sink into the heat
I wrap my body in the soap
working up a lather,
and close my eyes.

Stepping out of the tub
I glance at the mirror-
I am beautiful.

Bone structure chiseled into perfect symmetry
neck long and hard
shoulders broad with divine shape
the chest that others long for; wide and plentiful.
Stomach like the trails of the Adirondacks,
Smooth. Masculine.
I continue my journey.
I am long and wide,
Well endowed, not inherited by race, it just is.
Thighs muscular, damn near perfect.
Calves, large and solid
feet created for carrying such a work of art.

But then I open my eyes and look into the water
shocked by the reality hidden beneath the water's surface.

Isn't it deceiving what the night can do?

72 MINUTES

accomplishments ignored
failure brought to attention
life and death so abstractly viewed
secrets shared by mass population
scolded for knowing
bursting with intense frustration
into a mass of affliction

overhearing the one you love
premeditating your involuntary solidarity
gasping for air not because you're trapped
but because you have too much freedom
wanting to be held tighter, realizing
that it's your own hands around you

seeing your life flash in front you
at such a young age
being punished by ignorance… for stupidity
the words to the song no longer
making sense to you, now understanding
a dog's bark, more than the thoughts in your head

seeing an angel with the innocent white
feathered wing's take the innocence of small child
helplessness
being confused by confusion and
relating to silence

finally inhaling only to discover
there is no air left.
surrounded by people, inanimate, inadequate people,
only to feel alone
seeing the darkness of light, and of itself

tasting the bitterness of love
it's tangy ups and downs
biting into life only to learn
it's not well cooked, simply brown to the eyes

feeling your heart beat, knowing, hoping it's the last –
while one tear rolls down onto your lip, tasting this poem

JOURNAL ENTRY - NOT REALLY A POEM

I sit here observing the other patrons on the prowl, wondering why I'm alone. Am I waiting for someone? Am I longing for attention? Or, am I just that secure in my own skin that I dare pick through an appetizer of calamari and savor my perfect 10's – solo? I guess the answer is yet to be discovered.

It boggles them; one of only three Black men in the entire establishment; handsome, well-dressed, clearly sophisticated and ALONE. They wonder if I'm a top or bottom. Ha. I hate that fucking question - I mean, come on, can't you tell? My eyebrows arched and I'm rocking Timbs. I stand 6'1" and a solid 188 pounds, isn't it clear? Or, could I be a hustler looking for a trick? That would explain it all, right? I scan the room receiving a few suggestive glances, my body language reaffirms that it is not okay to approach me unless you're looking for a quick shutdown, now I become a bitch; a far cry from the fat kid in the bars holding up the wall while all my friends drank and danced their hearts out scouting for potential dates. I had no confidence back then, and shied away from anyone that feigned interest in me. I would've still been broke as hell if you would've paid me to go to a bar or club by myself.

I'm here in Boston's chic and trendy South end reading the local GLBT papers which just reiterates the same shit other GLBT papers read, just more or less Bay state specific. Our rights. Drag pageants. Balls. HIV ads. Safe sex ads. The L Word premier was a headliner. Pride. Pride. Pride. Don't get me wrong, I love a good read, but when the GLBT papers are our own Enquirer, why, as a gay man, as a Black gay man am I supposed to consider this substantial? I'm sure I just pissed someone off with that last comment; I mean how can I as a human being not consider HIV and safe sex ads substantial? Well, perhaps I'm just angry . Perhaps I'm tired of preachy ads that offer nothing but a single-sided view of the above topics. Perhaps I'm still uncertain as to why I can't open a heterosexual paper or magazine that show said ads. Perhaps, I'm over thinking it all.

So far I've fondled some calamari and a piece of grilled chicken flatbread, washing it all down with two glasses of Chardonnay and two perfect 10 martinis. Still no buzz - I'll research AA in the morning.

The crowd is mostly white men, many professional looking all with someone which is why the Black man typing away on his blackberry is bewildering. Ah, so what! I've been here before, not necessarily in this place, but in the same situation. I can't help this feeling of déjà vu. Since my youth, I've enjoyed my own company, especially on those occasions I need to think. Today was just one of those days. I'm trying to digest the absence of a particular 'love', telling myself I have already gotten over him.

I'm interrupted as I'm writing this, head down, drink in tow, by a slim, almost swimmers build white guy that takes the liberty of sitting across from me. I glance up, mainly because it was time to finish my cocktail. He smiles and asks who I'm texting? The smart ass in me wants to reply, but I hold him back and simply reply "it's private". I signal from my server and ask this time for a Grey Goose cosmopolitan straight up. He, the new suitor comments about how I'm no joke, and asks how many drinks I've had? At this point, I'm a bit confused as to why he's still within earshot and holding back my smart assed alter ego is becoming more difficult. I simply sigh, shake my head and finish these words. Then he utters words even I couldn't imagine. He (still unnamed) tells me how I'm the man of his dreams, and two things gave away that I had a big dick - I'm sitting here alone, and I'm Black. My friend could be held back the longer, and after some choice words my suitor and exited - stage left. I paid my tab, and seduced my drink. Then I left.

On the way home, I thought about what this guy said to me. Since when did being alone on a Friday night signify endowment? If anything, if I was the big dick Mandingo he imagined, shouldn't I have my choice of men? And are we still in the mindset that as a Black man, I am clearly *packing?* And besides, what is *packing?* Isn't that relative? This size queen in me thinks that you're not really packing until you're pushing upwards of 10 inches. To some, a simple 7 inches will intimidate, and what about thickness? Coke can or Italian sausage? It's all relative.

LIKE I'VE NEVER BEEN HURT

Broken emotions, irreparable with time
love that once flowed freely, now solidified.
A wounded heart trying so to hide,
fragile deep within, but not to the eye.

I gave you everything you took it all and more,
leaving nothing with hopes to restore.
Your selfishness left me cold; questioning others worth,
I want nothing more than to love like I've never been hurt.

There is a man who only wants to love,
and for me to love him in return,
but my hearts more comfortable with being hollow and frigid
then it is with being burned.

I can't seem to let him in not even a little, and
what's worse is with him I've got an all access pass
I can't turn my back on this opportunity to love,
who knows if this will be my last?

Hoping for love in your tomorrow,
when it's more than available today
can result in loneliness and regret,
both expensive prices to pay.

So I'm putting my pride aside, to live with the pains of yesterday

moving forward in love,

my heart reclaiming its turf,

loving me first, like I've never been hurt.

FOR NOW, FOREVER

I always fall for the wrong guys,
pretty boys who know they're pretty
young, dumb, and full of cum, and
ready to fill you with it.

I know they're not good for me,
but like carbs and fried chicken
I'm addicted to these boys, the ones that make me feel young, and
give me superficial hopes of the future.
They've got energy in bed, and are full of games, and
as many as I've been with, they're all the same
and although I'm looking for forever, I'm content with for now.

I search for them high and low,
ignoring the men I find in between
they can't hold me at night,
cause they're usually too weak, and
have to rush home to their roommates and their mamas.

I enjoy our time, even if it is a lie,
and look forward to tomorrow
our nights begin with drinks
and end the with a cigarette
truly fucked up since I don't smoke.

I shower them with gifts, leasing them for the moment
I try to show them a good time, with jazz and with wine,
but they only know the top 20 on the radio.

We're not even compatible to the blindest of eyes,
but when we hit the sheets, it's hip to thigh.
One takes the lead while the other follows
how deep is your love and how much will you allow?

The silly young boys that catch my glance,
the ones I know I shouldn't give a chance,
the foolish cuties so filled with drama
the ones lying to themselves as well as mama.
They come in and out of my life
like wings to a feather
fulfilling nothing more than my carnal desires
for now, for never.

REVERSAL OF ROLES

Hats off to you my baby,
you came into this situation
versatile but willing to give
of yourself entirely.

I've held back, afraid
but you know you have my heart,
my soul.
So tonight, it's yours.
Be sweet, but don't be gentle –
you got some making up to do.

It's yours baby, I'm ready to receive you
like you have night after night,
and in the mornings before work, and
sometimes on Sunday after church.

I've neglected those thick inches
leaving them in the cold, so
tonight, come on inside.
Stay warm.
I got a place for you
to lay your love.

Reach deep inside me, infinitely,

please me - like I hope I've been pleasing you.

Tonight your manhood is restored

and mine validated,

tonight, we become one.

COMMUNICATION

as I write this I feel

antiquated

as though I should be

key stroking these words

into a

BlackBerry

Palm

Pocket PC or

SK3.

jk. Lol.

oh what the hell

communication has

retro evolved

into fast fingers

and abbreviated words

the power of the pen

is no more

who needs a stamp

when we got

Evite

an e-mail

what do we say when we're

face-to-face

outside of the webcam

silence

we can't look into each other's eyes

there's no cursor there

baboons show their asses

when they desire to mate

us, we jump online and make asses of ourselves

SBM seeks SBM

6'1", 190 lbs

br/bk, mustache, goatee, full lips

9.5" cut – TOP.

fats/fems and other types need not respond

btw, no pic, no love.

clearly, this is all we need to know.

there is more to me.

more than I can fit into the 2000 characters

I'm allotted.

more than I'm willing for my cookies to collect

so some hacker can retrieve.

call me, let's talk, lol.

it's infectious you know

I can LMBOA too.

communicate with me,

like the good old days

you hang up first! No, you!

we started the shit.

I like you, do you like me too?

circle Y, N, or maybe.

that was the beginning of the end of communication.

Now we can't communicate.

If we could love with any gratification via text we would.

That's it.

Let's love emptily. Virtually.

ENOUGH

it wasn't until I was twenty-two
that I was okay with the
fact that I was never going to
be 6'2", with gray eyes and fair
skin, with what they consider "good" hair.
but, was I *Black* enough?

it wasn't until yesterday that
I was okay with the few extra pounds
I carry in my midsection.
and realized that no matter how hard I hit the gym,
ate fiber, and kale – cooked,
I'd never be fit enough.

I love to coo – coo with the girls,
and show my ass every now and then.
I'm out with my sexuality, but
still a man's man.
I'm a jock by some standards,
and a punk by others, but
I'm neither straight nor gay enough.

just this morning
while brunching on cooked salmon
cream cheese and capers,
with the coffee - black, and a doppio espresso on the side
sitting on the deck of my suburban home,

instead of bacon, eggs and grits

was I informed him that I wasn't *real* enough.

I was told that since I made my way out of the hood,

I'd forgotten where I came from.

I've learned to love my

Black,

thick,

gay,

bourgeois self -

flaws as abundant, yet concealed

as any day at 1600 Pennsylvania Ave.

the truth lies in

the heart, my heart

and I love

my. self.

LET ME KNOW

Kiss me.

Love me.

Hate me.

Resent me.

Reach out for me.

Forget me.

Forgive me.

Lay with me.

Walk away from me.

Hear me.

Listen to me.

Hold me.

Withdraw from me.

Yell at me.

Scream at me.

Roll your eyes at me.

Smack your lips at me.

Taste me.

Embrace me.

Know me.

Open up to me.

Tell me.

Show me.... some kind of damned emotions.

NIGHT AND DAY

the difference between night and day
is subtle, yet
what's allowed in the night
is forbidden in the day, and
what's allowed in the day is
taken for granted in the night.

our love, like night
and day
contrasts itself.
we love in the night
but are strangers in the day;
you take me to new heights
of ecstasy when the moon shines bright
but,
when the sun rises and
excites my awakening, you
like the moon
have vanished.

ON BEING CELIBATE

I pulled away from love
with no intention of
withdrawing from sex.
I never knew the two were one,
I'm horny but void of love.

So I become familiar with myself
inside and out.
The touch of my index finger as I circle
the thick head excites my shaft
with bloods necessary to
now demand the stroke of my entire hand.

I have to taste myself
and imagine that it's you.
Finger after finger, after finger
until…oooh…hsss.
In and out, strokin' up and down,
and out, and in and down and then

Being celibate, cleanup is easy,
and there's no one to scold me
for taking a draw from my Newport, and
there's no one to hold me
and say I love you – too
when you're celibate.

4 TO 714

I didn't know what normal was but
I knew when I heard that number – FOUR
it was not normal, or good.
I wish I could've
counted the tears that streamed from my eyes
as easily as *they'd* been counted.
Four.

I stared blankly - hearing nothing
more of the death sentence ahead of me.
Should I begin my goodbyes?
Would I even have enough time
to say what I wanted to say,
to whom I needed to say it to?
I felt limp and lifeless.
It was time to say goodbye.
Four.
That had to be wrong.
No one could be alive with just
four.
Denial.
I wasn't alive at all.

October 2002
the 19th day to be exact.
FOUR.
I wasn't fit to live.

FOUR.

I am not a quitter.

No way.

But how?

FOUR.

I found support in friends,

family, even coworkers.

I reached for God,

HE reached back.

I found my will

somewhere deep

in my heart,

and in God's presence

I found my will to live.

This, like the streets of Detroit

and the addicts I've been surrounded with

would

not

take

me.

I'm too damned evil

to succumb so easily.

FOUR IS NOT ENOUGH.

Normal 600+

Normal.

I've never wanted

to be normal.

No one could define normal

for me.

Society's acceptance?

Is that normal?

600+ is normal.

Today I am 714.

Never so proud to be "normal"

or to wear a number.

I am an individual, but

I embrace 714.

I've lost so many,

we all have - I almost lost myself.

No.

Not normal.

Better than.

Four

To

Seven hundred

Fourteen.

Thank

You

Jesus.

DETROIT (IN TWO VOICES)

My heart cries for you,
my city, once
the center of it all
now pegged
murder capital.
How could you?
How could you allow
yourself to deteriorate beyond control?
Beyond rebuilding?
How could you neglect your children,
providing them with what's now
the worse education system in the nation?
Detroit.

Your treasures
are hidden beneath the rubble, and
abandonment.
A slow rebirth.
Every forward step
your citizens knock you back, at least two.
You're filled
with gospel, and jazz
blues and soul
art and cuisine.
You're the automotive capital of the world - what happened?

You've segregated your many selves

nigga this, and nigga that -

I thought we buried that word.

I'm sorry I had to leave you,

but I am not a nigga,

and I refused to make you my bitch.

I wanted too much,

more than you were willing to provide.

Fuck you Detroit.

Fuck you

for letting this happen to us.

What about your black bottom

now an interstate under permanent construction?

South of 8 mile

shouldn't signify danger

and catastrophe.

Your people are leaving,

population declining

through murder

and migration.

I walk down your streets,

not nervous, cause this is home

always,

but sad.

We can't re-develop without

windows being broken

and graffiti.

Who the hell wants to invest in you

when you haven't invested in yourself?

Your reputation embarrasses me.
I'm a product of you but not a victim.
I am what you should be proud of,
but I had to go.
I'm sorry I abandoned you
like you abandoned me,
come back to me
Detroit.
I need you to be my phoenix –
resurrect yourself from
your own flames
come back to us
our sweet city,
my history is rooted
in your history.

I love you
Detroit, though you hated
and abandoned me.
I wasn't good enough
nor Black enough
careless enough
some say I'm not old enough
to remember what
you once were.

But I am you,
Detroit
and you
me.
You can take a man out of the city,
but you can't
take the city out of the man.

Detroit.

The strait.
The port of the Midwest.
Buildings that scrape skylines
a portrait of opportunity - failed.
Motown success -
music's biggest contributions.

My city.
Our city.
Motor city.
Abandoned city.

Detroit.

SCENT OF TWO

Yesterday, I was lying in bed
with the conundrum of aromas.
A complex duo of scents;
I should've straightened up before he arrived.

Now he's laying here in my arms
and you on my mind,
consumed and confused
with the perplexities
of each.
I should've changed the damned sheets.

Today, you arrived
unannounced
with a lust in your eyes.
You led me to the bed
the sheets were covered with sweat
from your skin, and
the oils of your hair, but
the scent of *his* sex filled the air.

Crazy over the smells
of you and him
I pounded you until my mind
and conscience were clear
but the scent of last night is still here

intermixed with versatility

the tops and bottoms

highs and lows of both nights.

This conundrum of scents is getting me high.

Tomorrow,

I insist on changing these damn sheets.

I can't go on with this charade of scents

any longer.

I'll go home to prepare for his arrival,

I'm excited at the thought of it

being just the two of us tonight.

I walked in the door

preparing to see my baby, but

not prepared to find the scents of two

together, in a compromising position

reaching heights of ecstasy

experimenting with chemistry,

creating a conundrum of musks

covering the sheets with oils

and the air with sex - without me.

Now I'm here overdosing

on the scents of three.

APARTMENT 5

Brick walls with eyes, hardwood floors
beaten with the paths of unrighteousness,
ooh, if only they could talk.
Things were different in Apartment 5
quiet in the day, but
alive with sin at night.
Apartment five was
a spacious two-bedroom
my own personal Studio 54.
Only the beautiful were admitted,
and what happened there,
stayed there – until now.
Apartment 5 filled with
disco queens, drag queens
threesomes, nights forgotten
how that bed and that deck
remained intact, nobody knows.
You found and lost yourself in
Apartment 5.
Worries left at the threshold, but like
muddy shoes, they were there
to greet you upon your exit.
You could be yourself, you could be anybody
if only for one night.
Generations of people, and
a shot of tequila to capture
every memory.

There was no segregation,
no inhibitions
in Apartment 5

My heart goes out to
apartments one, two, three, four and six.
I could call some of the nights
out by name
but in an attempt to protect the satisfied, and
exonerate the guilty - I won't.
What happened in Apartment 5
must stay in Apartment 5 and
in all of our wildest fantasies.

STAND

no matter how loudly we scream
our voices continue to be silenced by
temporary solutions and payoffs of
the status quo

our anger is taken lightly as
we become synonymous with settling
our pain, defused by broken promises of change
we've grown accustomed to this pain
after all, it's what has made *us* strong

we are blinded by instant gratification
our needs are manipulated
by society's needs
our screams denounced to a whisper

the blows of our oppressors are continuous
the stain remains and the bruises are only visible
to our ancestors
we become conditioned into Pavlov's canines
silenced on queue, salivating
for the purpose of entertainment and experimentation

let us continue our fight,
and be relentless in our pursuit to be heard
to be recognized, to be whole
let our forged silence speak

louder than their words

so loudly

let us find strength and

safety in numbers

we must stop tearing each other down

hold my hand brotha, lean on me sista

I got you, but

don't turn me away when I am weak

we're one

one heart

many tears

one voice

scream loudly

be silenced

no more

BLUE MORPHO

As he closes his wings
so wide and so free,
he appears to be as
ordinary as you and me.

So he sits there still
like the breath I breathe,
his next move determined
by how you react.

Treat him kind, even
grace him with love, and
he'll share his secret as he soars
above the world so shallow
so cruel, and untrue
to reveal his other side
so royal and blue.

Judge not a book it's cover
as plain as it may seem,
but open your mind and you'll discover
a wondrous world, like that
of a butterfly's wings.

NATURE'S COURSE

Anguish consumes my days
and I have no time to live
a soaring eagle unable to take flight.

Sorrow residing in my heart
as I dare to look in
the face of reality - so harsh and unreal.

The taking of a dolphins fin
leaving it to drown
on the ocean's floor.

Simply a carcass for scavengers to prey upon
a million memories, a million cries, lies and kisses
all taken away.

WANTING

A caged bird with and
held captive by a loves rejection
yearning only to be loved
while loathing his reflection.

Caught in the spell, bound by tears
afraid and tormented by circumstance,
yet guarded by fears.

Kept company by sorrow, conversing with hope
with desperation against despair
he's trying to cope.

Reminiscing on yesterday, and
the good times,
keeping warm with echoing caged bird rhymes.

NO MORE

no more kisses in the morning
no more notes while I'm gone
no more wishful thinking tears
no more sad I love you songs.

no more reluctance to live
no more waiting for your call
no more willingness to give
no more scared to fall.

no more looking back on yesterday
no more candles burning dim
no more putting you ahead of me
no more 'I need him'.

no more putting me aside
no more making you happy first
no more dying for a drink
only to quench your thirst.

no more wondering what the future holds
no more sad and lonely poems
there's no more rain in my forecast
no more, cause I'm moving on.

BLACK BUTTERFLY - A TRIBUTE TO DENNIS

So precious and rare,
a jewel undiscovered, but
available to the world.
Don't worry love - I notice you.

An angel, silent
without sound
the flutter of your wings
assure me that everything is alright.

Black, silken, sown lace
my muse, my energy
one-of-a-kind and you're mine - all mine.
Fly butterfly, your destination is eternal life.

Soar - free willing and you'll
never be captured.
Land on me and replenish me with love.
My heart, my world is desolate without you,
fly, and fill me with hope.

Cry butterfly, you have emotions too
laugh butterfly
sing butterfly with your melodic notes
love butterfly, love me
live butterfly, live for you
camouflage yourself with laughter.

Be reborn butterfly.

God gave you metamorphosis.

Re-create yourself, into yourself

finally.

POEMS AND OTHER RANTS

BECAUSE IT MATTERS TO ME

He's not afraid to buy children's books
remembering they were once my muse
he sends random cards that are blank inside
filling them with partial truths.

He encourages me to meditate
refusing to allow this world to take me down
he whispers words I long to hear
without even making a sound.

He hears and listens to what I say
without hanging on my every word -
not afraid to tell me the truth.
He asks how my day was and listens purposefully,
he does these things because they matter to me.

He travels great distances to be a face in the crowd
he gets excited about simple things, comfortable with his inner child,
he includes me on decisions, when I should have absolutely no say
trying to see things the way that I see
he does so because it matters to me.

He likes drive thru food, and cheap wine
and pretends to love the gym
he lays 'on bed' for a midday nap
when I insist we keep going
he buys coffee for the house but he prefers tea
he does so, because it matters to me.

He laughs at my jokes
deals with my moods
allowing me to simply be,
he cries my tears
feels my pain
carries my burdens while shouldering his.

I mentioned in a whisper one Thursday night
he listened intently, taking notice of my worries
never using my hang-ups against me.

He said on the same night
'you care for and protect those close to you,
who do you allow to keep you safe?'

One evening when I turned cold
because he was getting too close
demanding that he leave
he packed his bags and left his love
because that love mattered to me.

BOY BLUE

eyes heavy

burdened, bruised

heavy load bearing

hollow laughter, shielding questions

oh, how he wants someone, anyone

to ask this question.

we must know better

for if we ask he might just pour it all out

spill what he's been hiding,

unload what he's been carrying,

yet still leave our question unanswered.

boy blue, with grown man blues

silences himself to avoid the pain

he poses for us but we can't see

beyond his double-take beauty

unconcerned with the love and pain inside.

boy blue had no other choice,

he was surrounded by emptiness

suffocating from Christian expectations

set forth by the lips that at one point whispered *son*

the last words heard from those lips – *sinner*.

now I lay me down to sleep

I pray the Lord my soul to keep

if I should die before I wake

I pray the Lord my soul to take

boy blue among the sky

the rustle in the autumn leaves

the laughter of children all around

a loving life ended all too soon because of Christianity.

boy blue

boy unknown

boy loved

boy gone too soon

CATASTROPHE

I wonder what would happen if
offshore drilling and rigs exploded off
the coast of Cape Cod, Martha's Vineyard,
Nantucket or East Hampton.

Do you think America or the world
would react differently?

If Maine lobsters weren't so alive and kickin'
and northern fishermen were fighting to thrive
would America fight harder for its people
wildlife and wetlands to survive?

If the winds stirred up, or
the ground began to shake in the concrete jungle
would Madison Square Garden be filled
with displaced residents from 5th Avenue,
or is the ninth Ward and Superdome more equipped?

Would decaying bodies pile up
in the summer sun
or flow lifelessly
along the banks of the Hudson's run?

What would happen if the classist elite
were suddenly in need
if the donors to political parties were displaced,
would things have happened differently?

If the faces of pain, anguish,
and displacement were freckled and pale,
if the eyes of uncertainty blue,
if there were strands of blond hair on beheaded heads,
what do you think America would do?

If the topic of debate was whether
Europeans were allowed entry
into this land of opportunity
would we need 2500 pages of a minority report
to dispute it?

If AIDS had begun as a straight disease,
would we preach about it in our churches,
cry from our pulpits
and demand education and change?

Or, would modern day Christian terrorism
remain the same?

This is a poem for the privileged elite,
who are oblivious to their husbands dicking their sons,
for the religious zealots in Uganda and abroad
speaking more fluently about sodomy
and gay relations than any sissy I know.

This is a poem for politicians in America,
so afraid to have opinions of their own,
a poem for the underserved, underprivileged
underrepresented with so much to say,
and for the almighty dollar, losing its value every day.

This is the poem that keeps me up at night
when the aforementioned sleep peacefully,
this is the poem that wasn't written by me
instead, it was written by this
bullshit ass, self-made, worldwide catastrophe.

CONFESSIONS

I confessed something tonight
wrote you an e-mail, came clean
scattered thoughts kind of like poem
I confessed something tonight.

Told you about all my issues
laid it all on the line
gave you every chance to leave
every reason to hate me
I confessed something tonight.

Wrote it down like journal entries
then left the book open
listened to you flip through the pages
waiting, hurting for what was to come next
I confessed something tonight.

I put my trust in another
gave him me
told him to leave
run
run far
run fast
while he still can.
He said 'I read your e-mail'
then
he confessed something tonight.

Told me he loved me still
told me he loved me more
said, I know your hurt
I cry your tears
he confessed something tonight.

He told his story, much like mine
eerie similarities
much like meant to be
he confessed something tonight.

He spoke about love
spoke about hate
about resentment
and family
of death
he confessed something tonight.

He said I love you,
to me and to himself
I said I love you
to him and to myself
we confessed something tonight.

I AM (AN EGO TRIP)

I am the one you're drawn to
without knowing why,
I am the stutter in your speech, and
the twinkle in your eye.

I am your turbulent flight,
safe landing and first class upgrade,
I am the largest float
in your everyday parade.

I am your shame-filled addiction
halfway house and rehabilitation,
I am the uncertainty of your day, and
your evening meditation.

I am your bedroom fantasy,
your Facebook stalk,
I am your blackboard with
permanent chalk.

I am your top, your bottom,
your Black pride.
I am the temporary paralysis
in your left thigh.

I am your platoon sergeant,
your final recruit,
I'm your sweet and sour -
your forbidden fruit.

I am your skydive, bungee jump
parasail and scuba gear
I'm your yesterday, tomorrow
far and near.

I am your Moodswings,
your cloudy judgment,
I'm your extravagant living
and your check to check budget.

I am your alliance formed,
your anti-norm,
your wish you could,
your misunderstood.

I am your pedestal, and
your noose,
I am your back of the closet denial, and
your truth.

I am what I was back then
and more importantly what I am now,
I am the where, the who, the when
the why and how.

I am the one I've been waiting for
but afraid to receive,
I am my own spiritual awakening
that's hard to believe.

I am your pocketbook, your stilettos
Timbs and throwback crunk,
I'm your polyblend suit, favorite silk tie
I'm the pep in your step and the tears that you cry.

I am your morning cup of coffee,
taken black or with cream,
I can be taken in or let out
just like an inseam.

I am your nocturnal emission,
your life altering decision,
I'm your patented invention, and
your number one Twitter mention.

I am your Epiphany,
your **A HA** moment,
I'm your black tie affair and
your block party showman.

I am your father, your brother,
your lover your friend,
I am your purgatory,
your beginning and end.

I am your PS3, your Nintendo WII,
your Gameboy and Atari.
I'm your favorite CD, your MP3, your DVD, Blue Ray HD and your rabbit-eared t.v.

I am the childhood memory,
that lived under your bed,
I'm the one you can't seem to
get out of your head.

I am your Easybake oven,
your Barbie dream house,
I'm your G.I. Joe and
Mighty Mouse.

I am the original Slinky,
oh what a wonderful toy,
I can be stretched for miles, and
I'm fun for a ....boy.

I am your complicated,
your overrated,
your people's poet, and
ALL should know it.

I am your speak and tongues,
that air in your lungs
your sexual innuendo
your symphonic decrescendo.

I am your daffodil,
your calla lily,
your thugged-out nigga, and
your hillbilly.

I am the monster you make me out to be, and
an angel in disguise,
I'm the one you hate to love,
and try to despise.

I am both your diagnosed disease, and
your cure,
I am your ONE MAN show
on this 80 city tour.

I am your pain, your pleasure
your ecstasy beyond measure.
I'm your violent temperament, and
your favorite night time
under the sheets all by yourself instrument.

I am your night sweats,
your cry me to sleep,
I'm your thought provoking,
sensitive shallow and deep.

I am your FUCK YOU for the cause, and
let's hold hands and pray,
I'm your picket lines, and
your marriage equality act, and repeal Don't Ask Don't Tell signs.

I am your every season,
your make believe in,
I'm your beg your pardon, and
your early morning hard on.

I am your Pharaoh, your King,
your Nile running deep,
your Yimmy ya, and Kumbaya
I am your Audre Lorde and your Barbara Jordan.

I am your dependency, your cope,
your reach for me rope.
I am your inner-city gutter, and
your bread and butter.

I am your infinity,
your A - Z
I'm your voice within and
your un-repented for sins

I'm a shy boy from the Midwest,
your Sunday's best,
I am…. aww fuck it,
I'll let you figure out the rest.

FOR THE BOYS

For the boys online looking for love
on adam 4 adam or Black gay chat
with their dick pic profile shots
and their mannequin modelesque stats

For the boys in the clubs looking for love
sipping overpriced drinks with their
pinkies pointing north, or sandwiched between
strangers feeling complete, sans the empty
feeling that consumes them.

For the boys in the parks, who don't
really get down like that saying I only let
niggas suck my dick, and occasionally
I'll fuck a dude, but I ain't gay.

For the lonely little boys who only need daddy's love
praises for making straight A's
muted from being chastised
for not being able to throw a ball.

For the boys so afraid of loneliness
and not being accepted that they make excuses
for the repeated meetings
with their eye and a lover's fist.

For the boys, turned men, always boys
who fail to look inside for wholeness and completion
because we don't teach our little boys their truth,
we garner them with intangible expectations,
repeatedly resurrected by history's score.

Patriarchal fallacies, like grinding gears
intermittent drops of water – blackboards and nails
unbearable and persistent.

For the boys who have been wounded
by love, lies and circumstance
stand in your truth!

Venomous words, condemning slurs
heavy fists and an occasional kick throw at you
STAND. Endure the pain of a thousand paper cuts,
with grains of salt in each wound – healed by truth.

For the boys looking outward,
pliable in their beliefs to gain the affection – look inside
where it's been all along.

For the boys who can barely speak above a whisper
plant your feet in your truth, and
in the soil of your own love.

HURTING

I told you two books ago, page 36 during one of my *Mood Swings* that I
only know how to love
one way… hard with everything in me
wanting to be your everything
and your nothing.
you laughed me off, thought it was some poets way of filling a page
and you, like readers abroad missed the message.
I continued to write, poem after poem, book after book,
even dedicated one to you, hoping that would
inspire you to read the words beyond the dedication,
we argued instead.
found fault in each others' differences.
I grew exhausted with the tension in the house we share,
so I gathered the best hemp I could , and smudged the place,
hoping to rid the space of the negative spirits, but then
I heard your key in the door.

I traveled around to get to know me, and forget you
and I found solace in strangers.
men that spoke the words you never did, the very
words I'd asked to hear fight after fight after fight.
they spoke these words to me, as if they'd read my journal
entered my mind, rested on my heart synching with each beat.
with the introduction to every stranger, I forgot you more and more
but you were still there when I came home.
you reached for me, I pulled away.
said I can't be held by a stranger; the irony.

I saw the hurt in your eyes, now, years too late you want to talk.
me with my skilled play on words had nothing to say.
the hurt in your eyes was more than I could bear to watch,
but all the ammunition I needed.
I wanted you to hurt the way I hurt.
you became the perfect man, the one I asked for
time again, but I could see the exhaustion growing
in your face as you strived to be something unfamiliar.

I grew cold and indifferent, not knowing whether to hurt you
with the truth or with a lie, but I knew I wanted to, needed to hurt you.
so I left you be, while you struggled to flip the pages of my epiphany
learning more about me.

Kelly Clarkston sang, *"I didn't come here to hurt you now I can't stop"*
these words play over and over in my head,
I didn't come here to hurt you now I can't stop
I didn't come here to hurt you now I can't stop
I can't stop hurting you with my lies
I can't stop hurting you with my truth
I can't stop hurting you with my distance
I can't stop hurting you with my indifference
I can't stop hurting you with words
I can't stop hurting you until you feel
the pain I felt for so long
the pain you insisted was me being sensitive
the pain you ignored.
I can't stop hurting you until you feel
the pain you didn't even cause.
I open my mouth to say the words you

don't want to hear, but need to be spoken
but the pain in your eyes is too much for this
jaded and conflicted heart to take.
I didn't come here to hurt you now I can't stop.
I didn't come here to hurt you, now I can't stop.
I didn't come here to hurt *me*, but I can't stop.

POETRY

1.

poetry. found. me.

when it (my heart) was dark.

when I was scared. when I was alone.

it (poetry) grabbed me as I jumped.

held on tight. refused to let go.

me dead weight.

poetry – infinitely strong

grabbed me like the gospel

does Christians.

talked me off a ledge.

placed paper and a crippled

pencil in my hand – said go.

write it all down.

when I fought hard , even refused

poetry struck a nerve.

reminded me of pain

abuse

scorn

torment

violent speech and

like sulfur and tar

excited a reflex.

made me purge and vomit

the words onto paper

and deaf ears.

said see now, that's all better

I rocked violently and
poetry let me be –
said shhh, there there.

2.

poetry.
called me again to do
what the ancestors
instructed me to do.
said I must tell my story.
who will listen?
said I must tell their stories.
they've already been told.
said I must tell our stories.
I couldn't argue.
but, I'm tired.
no, you're selfish.
be restless and go forth.
if you don't tell it
our story will be twisted
misconstrued and misused.
where do I begin?
where you left off.
I began to save lives,
like mine was saved
by poetry.

3.

poetry / is / like / water
poured itself into my heart
spilled a little on my shirt
for everyone to notice
quenched my thirst.
people pointed and laughed.
had opinions
people came close
people ran away
but no one read
the words, or
beyond the words
instead they thought
little of
poetry / verse
poetry / lyric
poetry / play on / words
mine / yours
ancestral
over / underrated
live saving
poetry.

PATIENCE

I am writing this as I'm waiting. I'm waiting to meet someone for lunch, I'm waiting for a phone call from that same someone. I'm waiting for a table in Starbucks to open up close to an outlet so that I can work. I'm waiting to hear back about a book proposal. I'm waiting on a refund check, I'm waiting on my bus to arrive, I'm waiting… and then something grabs my attention. I look up at all the other visitors gawking at a hole. A mere construction site, or is it? I'm waiting to find out what the fuss is all about and then, I slow down, pay attention and read. I'm standing on Ground Zero. This feeling comes over me and I can't breathe. I call my friend in Detroit who was with me when tragedy struck, and I can't talk. All of a sudden I can smell the flames and feel the bodies given no other choice but to descend from what were once buildings above. I'm covered in ash and rubble and history, and I am patient.

Eight years ago there stood two magnificent structures directing the world's monetary movement; eight years and twenty-two days ago the world stopped turning. Like slavery, it seems these locals have forgotten what was ever here, while us visitors stand mouths agape in remembrance. I am blessed. September 11th began my ever continuing lesson on patience, and prayer. I sit here numb, waiting still but unaware of it all. It's not important to me anymore. I am not important to me anymore. Construction workers handed insurmountable responsibility of reconstructing something irreplaceable. I am thankful.

Brown bagged lunches
reminiscent of grade school days.
Sitting on green marble

semi-circles starring at blankness.

Pondering everything, knowing nothing.

How history changes things.

How history repeats and remains unremembered.

Cool winds, September

Ash and soot, chimney swept

But the memories linger.

Breath taken,

Lives shaken.

Missed goodbyes

Endless cries

Here today

Gone tomorrow

A world torn

A country mourns

Gone to war

And what for?

Still fighting,

Still dying

Senseless then

Careless now.

WAKE UP CALL

A kiss upon my necks nape
somewhere between the confusion
of the moon going into hiding
and the days break.

I could feel his heat behind me
as his arms pulled me into him.
We fought sleep all weekend much
like we pretended to fight this feeling.
But, just as exhaustion reveals itself
this connection, too, was evident.

It was sudden to us both, but calculated
and prepared for.
I could feel the beat of his heat against
the sweet of my, mmm.

Turned over on back, him
Knees bent, contact made - eyes that is.
Staring into, at each other's naked eyes,
Telling, revealing, vulnerable eyes
Shaped like, shaded like espresso bean eyes.

His microfiber suede soft lips
touching the spots they learned over
the weekend that I like.
Eyes disconnected now, body conjoined vibes like harmonious chords.

Hips relaxed and welcoming him
into me.
He smooth sailed his way inside - mind wise, like
he belonged there.
Like he was home after a long day's work,
and I had dinner laid out and a bath drawn - not
like 51 hours ago he did not know my name, and I couldn't care less about
his.

Back arched,
neck snapped,
hips gyrating,
eyes rolling
exorcism type shit, but
let's not rebuke or refuse this,
I ain't sure 'bout shit except,
I need him here inside.

I could feel him swell
as he laid his pound of flesh
where few others have dwelled.
Excited by his new discovery
he began to throb, unable to
contain himself so with
little notice he let himself in
and no one has ever felt so familiar
so welcome, so at home, so real.

If blood could make its way there
It was erect, even my goose bumps

had goose bumps.
And while we discovered the layout of
the room, the phone rang -
**"This is the front desk with your 4:30 am
wake up call."**
He never removed himself
from me or the situation, answering the
phone with a sedated rhythm and no hesitation.

Me grabbing the headboard, then
the wall, finally the sheets -
He pulled me to the edge I held
On to him and this feeling, as he raced
Not that sloppy amateur pace, that
Look behind you I'm about to pass you twice,
but it's proper etiquette to
speed up this close to the finish line
type niceness where I could
still feel the inches of his thickness
and the rhythm of his drum beat.
And then the crescendo, kind of like
Forzando, and the melody lingered on.

This was my 4:30 am wakeup call - no
need to hit snooze, I was frozen in place and time
reluctant to leave – but nothing lasts forever.
I wish we could go back to this time when
it was just me and you, you and me -
When we were able to drown out the noise
of others with the beat of our hearts

and the silence of our gaze.

But we were overcome by distance

and circumstance and the past

and now, each day without your voice

your embrace and your love is

my every day wake up call.

HE MAKE ME WRITE POEMS

He make me write poems…
Not heart broken, miserable teary-eyed poems,
He make me write poems like… love.

We sat up and talked, spoke, spake,
To each other about he, about me, about life, like…
Chaos and dysfunction and the
Element of surprise like…

When two people meet in the middle of the sea
Amongst heat, and waves and strangers, masses of
Chaos and disorder.

Introductions formal like, M.I.S.T.E.R.
Mouth filled with buttery biscuits
Caught off guard with him, by him.

He make me write poems even I don't understand, like…
Why my mind can't rid itself of thoughts of this man.
It feels so good to write a poem not in anger, or hurt but
In hope like…

Saving your allowance for a new pair of skates and
Sailing across the veneered surface for the first time
Without… falling down.
He make me write poems unfamiliar, like…
The feeling I got the first time his lips touched mine.

He make me write poems about normalcy, and consistency
Like…
Big mama's deep fried chicken and how the sun always
Rises in the east and sets in the west.

Like nature, natural is what I felt when my eyes closed,
and
I exhaled.
Muscles relaxing, yin / yang love type chi.

He make me write poems…
Sweet, melodic, smile like poems
That with time will polish this tarnished
History bruised heart.

He make me write poems like…
                                      Like….
                Like…
Like…

Waking up before going to sleep
Like….
Like….
Like…
Only he can… like…
Only he has.

ON SELF LOVE

Damn, I must've been about 26 or 27 when I made the decision to start loving me. For two and half decades my native tongue was "YOU". You this. You that. YOU, YOU, YOU. My everyday behaviors were focused around society, my family, my friends, my job, school ... *my relationships.*

I was under this false impression that by making other people happy, I would eventually find happiness myself. I couldn't have been more wrong. I was 18 the first time I found *love*, or so I thought. I met a dude. A lil' shorty. Smooth talker. Deep penetrating eyes, and like me he wrote poems. He was a sexy lil' kat. Seemed real comfortable with who he was; had swag ya know? He paid me attention. You see, I was this fat kid, band geek, honor student. I mean I was cool; I had my share of friends, but inside I hurt deeply. The image in the mirror was more than I could stand looking at. So, you see when this kat came along, I thought he was bullshittin'. No way lil' shorty could be into me! We spent long nights on the phone, and started skipping class to chill at his place. It was nice. He was my first. Now, I had messed around with dudes before. A little foreplay and shit, but this guy was the first man I explored inside and out. After that, I was gone. I lost myself in yet another. He was the first man besides my father to hurt me, and… he was also the last. I gave him the permission to hurt me by putting him, before me. He saw the naïve little kid that hurt for attention and affection and this … this dude definitely used it to his advantage. It's funny what happens when you give a motherfucker control over your life!

I never thought love was for me, so I was never afraid of getting hurt. I always had girlfriends, so on some level I was always detached. I knew I was gay. I mean, I was sneakin' peeks at dudes dicks when my moms was covering my eyes on some lame ass sex scene on T.V. I was never looking at titties dancing up and down, but my moms was none the wiser. I think that's why I was always detached – I knew it wasn't for me, but it was what was expected of me. Again, living for someone else.

Anyway, I guess karma really is a bitch cause the first time I truly loved, I got hurt.

I was always scared to kick it with guys. I mean people were talking about AIDS like it was the next big fad. Dudes in prison were contracting it, commercials preached abstinence, *it* was God's "punishment" for homosexuality.

My hard-headed ass, despite the warning, despite the stuff I already knew, despite the facts, despite the ignorant messages, because of "love", with this kat he wanted it raw, and I obliged. Reluctantly, but hey that's love or what I thought was love.

Love, by definition is:

- A strong affection for <u>another</u> arising out of kinship or personal ties
- Attraction based on sexual desire?
- An unselfish loyal and benevolent concern for the good of <u>another</u>

Love, by my definition is A BITCH!!!

I mean, at what point, and where are we instructed to love ourselves, to be unselfish to me / us ???

The Bible says love thy neighbor the way that Christ loved you… honor thy mother, honor thy father. Where does the good book give us permission to love ourselves?

Thirty – one years…. and I'm still learning. It's a trip 'cause people look at me like I'm speaking Arabic when I say ME time, or without apology put ME first. I said YOU for so long it's like ME is my second language, and I'm still not fluent.

Well, I'm still learning. Like adopting any second tongue, I practice everyday. I've learned the people that are truly down for me along the way. I'm working on it. I'm working on me, and I'm here.

WE ARE

(a poem for Alicia and Thiadora)

We are strangers who met once
In a world so far away,
And when our eyes locked again in that same great place
With each other is where we knew we must stay.

We are a collage of colors nestled
On the hills serene landscape,
We are beginning a new journey
On our everyday.

We are the face of love
Staring back at adversity
We are each others, and
Our own new beginning.

We are the love song that
We loved to dance, but
Until we found each other
We danced it alone.

We are the shelter that protects us
When the world rears its ugly head,
Ah, but alas, we are the ones
Who no longer know alone.

We are a conundrum of flavors
Masterfully selected as one,
Individual and distinct –
Lingering on the palate of love.

We are the hands that wipe away one another's tears,
Even when it's the tears we cause,
We are the ones who've accepted each other
In spite of our own flaws.

We are the careless whispers in the wind,
And the regimented structure of the day,
We are the ones who point each other north
When the other has lost their way.

We are the countless number of days ahead
Filling each one with love
And when time or distance separates us
You'll be the one I'm thinking of.

And when today has been one big blur,
And tomorrow does not seem so new
I'll find solace in knowing that
I'm coming home to you.

I'll reach for you without knowing,
Exception or hesitation,
Because my love for your surmounts
Any fears or trepidation.

And while the days ahead we can't sketch out
and make perfect in our own ways,
know that I'll be there at the beginning, and
at the end of each of those days.

Ready to hold you and receive you,
Or to just let you be.
Because, this I promise to you, and
This you promise to me.

We are no longer strangers, and
In some sense we never were,
Because the Creator produced her for me,
And created me for her.

We are merely the ones we've been waiting for
For all of our lives, and
On this day, and forever more
We shall be known as wives.

MINDFUCK

I have to travel with you
Airport security scan/bag check/contraband
and I have to explain *no sir, those are just my meds*
doctors note/side effects/warning labels

Icebreaker includes, well, let's see
I'm 31, live alone, some say I'm an artist and...
There's this hesitation
should I/shouldn't I like
he loves/he loves me not.

Healthy living minus the daily reminder
that this pill, these pills – cocktail.
Remember when cocktails used to be fun?
Out on the town with your besties
sipping on *cocktails*, my cocktail is now
"take one tablet daily at bedtime".

May cause drowsiness, or nausea
headache and fatigue
do not operate heavy machinery –
like what; my dildo?
May cause upset stomach, vomiting
and in most cases diarrhea.
Side effects include depression,
as if living with/dying from this isn't
depressing enough.

Do not take with alcohol – oh well
this is not the drug for me.

An oblong pink pill is my daily mindfuck,
warping my beliefs into thinking
normalcy is within reach.
Never knowing the intimacy of
bringing a life into this world
unable to justify why I
as the last standing male in my family
cannot carry on the family name.

I listen to close-minded mutherfuckers
talking about hugging, kissing and shaking hands.
Look at that nigga, skinny and shit - yo he look sick.
Rumors spreading like wildfire, destroying lives
HE is trouble.

I don't look like your stereotyped
rag and bones
lesion sporting
he brought this upon himself
what must he have done wrong
to end up like this
fatigued, yellow eyed
emaciated
western blot rejected
clinic visiting
goodbyes saying
final resting place planning
ignorance.

I stand to my feet, extend my hand
pull a stranger close; whisper
I am living; however inconveniently
with inconvenient HIV.

Now you have just been mindfucked.

ON SAYING GOODBYE

Sometimes hello is harder than goodbye; making the decision to let someone into your life, whether you've been subject to pain in the past or not can be difficult. Bringing someone, be it a new friend, potential love, a mentor, doctor etc. into your mess can yield many wonderful outcomes, or many trying times. It has been said that when we let someone into our lives just close enough, we are subconsciously giving them the green light to hurt us. I know that sounds strange, and perhaps a bit sadistic but think about it; opening up to that degree gives people the tools required to turn things around on you. Your fears, weaknesses, worries, painful memories, dirty laundry can all be used to cause *you* pain.

Now, goodbye however; we look at goodbye as this awful thing, this forever, this we did something wrong when in reality goodbye is an amazing thing. Goodbye opens up doors and brings refreshing energy and light that can sometimes be incomprehensible. A good friend of mine, Minister Byron Jamal said to me at our first meeting when he barely knew my last name, as he looked in his rearview mirror *"my brother, you have to be as faithful in letting go as you are and holding on"*. Now Byron didn't know what I was going through at that moment, nor have I told him to this day that his words, those words could not have come at a more appropriate time. You see I was involved in a relationship where I still struggled with being honest about my feelings and holding onto something I knew would not last. I was relentless and faithful in my holding on although it caused unhappiness, but I was hesitant, fearful, reluctant, and handicapped by being able to say goodbye. What I've learned since then is my utter selfishness; while in my heart I was doing the right thing, I was holding someone back from finding the potential love that I know in my heart they deserve, that I was unwilling and incapable of giving.

My advice to anyone out there struggling with letting go is simply this; write a list of all the people in your life beginning with the one or the ones involved in your struggle with letting go and ask yourself how many of these people, who on this list wakes up with the sole intention of making you happy? I guarantee if you're being completely honest with yourself you will find that no one, probably not even your parents and definitely not the one you think you love wakes up asking themselves how they can make you happy today. If this doesn't make your decision any easier, I don't know what will.

A DEEPER LOVE

they said I couldn't be me
wrapped their façade around my true self
trying to hide me
they put their words into my mouth and
I choked. I choked on the lies, the commonality
the bullshit even they didn't believe

they tried to people my dreams
p.c. my speech, rob me of my ethnic superiority
my beauty, even straighten my wrist
at the command of the sway and my hips,
stood in the truth of my blackness and
moved beyond and above the paralysis
of the history of the path they set for me

the freedom of my expression is liberating
giving thanks to my ancestors, paying it forward
to my future.
the truth of your expression is in your pride
and this is your platform, the world is your stage
breathe life into your individuality
embrace and flaunt your sexuality
vomit up your insecurities
emerge beyond your obscurities
dismiss the churches shunning of your *impurities*
rely on the love that*'s* inside of thee.

dispel the myths around your inevitable Blackness, and
your born-again queerness
rise above this should not, and could not
give society back all their isms
and express your authentic self
be audacious and unapologetic in your truth.

TOKEN

Don't be a bengal me around your wrists
Nor flaunt me to your friends
I cannot accessorize your political correctness,
nor can I add that extra *umph*
to your rainbow circle of calculated diversity.

It's true my Blackness is beautiful
but it belongs to me,
it can't be draped across your shoulders
to don your social conscious mentality.

I'm glad you voted for Obama, but
what did you do it for?
To mend the broken nation that
your people stole and have owned for years, or
to be the forward-thinking non-conformist
amongst your elitist peers?

Don't attempt to slide your soul into me
to achieve a perfect fit
I cannot carry you up to forward thinking
across sand dunes of gender inequality
nor can I make up for the inadequacies
of history's past, and rationalize today's
overcompensation.

You must ensure that tomorrow is different.

I won't dance in your tribal circle of coonery
nor engage in your agenda of silly faggotry.
Take the limited vocabulary of these jokes and slurs
to your sideshow counterparts, and...
dissect them.

Invade and analyze the why and how,
the cause and effect, the damage.
Place the root cause under a lens at 400x
and be taken away by the anguish my people have known.

You say you want to get to know me
that you're intrigued by my feminist forward thinking
captivated by my artistic approach on not artistic issues
you marvel at my passion and energy around the *cause*.

Don't categorize me as your status quo
nor coin me as your gay Black friend
don't bejewel me with ethnic beads you've collected
from your travels to great distant lands
don't hang me on your walls as the art you're proud of
symbolizing your five-star all-inclusive resort gift shop dreams
don't banner me in your annual parades
collecting front-page photo ops that you clip and save
don't paint a smile on my face because of my progression
ignoring centuries of pain that can't be erased.

GRANDMA'S POEM

(a poem for Mary)

The words I never said
because I thought you always knew,
are simply I wouldn't be the man you've been proud of all your life
if it had not been for you.

You mustered up the courage
to raise a second child -
a product discarded in the exchange of drugs,
living your life all the while.

You called me your second chance -
redemption for mistakes made before,
I wanted to be the epitome of you
from the core of my core.

You showered me with love unconditional
breathing into me new life,
while these are the words I've never said
but have always known inside.

Now I sit here and watch you suffer
your pain I can feel,
our breaths are staggered together
the hurt, synched – is undeniably real.

You named me your soul mate
an understatement by far,
and as I ready myself to let go
a part of me will surely die.

The values you've instilled in me
I will forever carry on,
but after 32 years of having you by my side
I'm afraid to do this alone.

You said you've been here many times before
no doubt you'll be here again,
this morning you left me for good and
found your place in heaven
amongst the angels who called you home
in the place made especially for you.

Each day is a new pain
an empty unjustified adventure,
but I press on for you, to continue your legacy
because you wouldn't have it any other way.

Of all the words in all the world
I cannot describe the pain,
it's beyond hurt, agonizing to my soul
heart stopping anguish.

I feel you in everything around me
the voices of children, sounds of nature
even the female pilot you never met.

I see you when I think I've escaped dangers
or when I hear your favorite song;
in pointed middle fingers, and sharp tongues
in rolled eyes and the scolding of children
in homemade peanut butter fudge
fried chicken and Grandma Annie's chili
in white wine and German beer
at the kitchen table that will never be the same again
in the face of your granddaughter; a beautiful woman
in the heart of your daughter – so strong.
Your presence is in the waves around me
the life in the air I breathe
I hurt so hard and unexpected
for woman I thought would never leave.

I know it sounds silly to say
but, I thought you would never die
I can call our memories out by name
date stamped with only your smile
it seems like you've been gone forever
and it's only been a short while
I pick up the phone to call you,
bought you a card the other day
addressed to a place in heaven
because I had so much to say.

I know this poem makes no sense
neither does the bond we share
people don't understand the void I feel
but I forgive them because they weren't there.

I long for the day we meet again
holding fast to the memories I keep
I've lost my energy in weary times
my confidant and my muse
these words I thought I'd never said
are the words I hope you knew.
The world called you wildcat, fire, and strength
the world was right
I call you every day every thing, all I knew
and now you're gone from my sight.
It's a challenge to carry on your legacy
to find the strength I'll never have
to live in the shadow of absolute greatness
of a woman adored.

The words I feel like I've never said, but
hope you always knew, are
you are my best friend, my soul mate
and I'd be nothing without you.

URIAH BELL, author of *epiphany: poems in the key of love* is a poet, author, public speaker and activist. *Mood Swings 2nd ed* is a re-release of Uriah's first collection of poems with 20 new pieces. *Mood Swings* is an emotionally raw journey that explores sex and sexuality, racism, gender identity, and HIV. Uriah currently resides in Boston, MA. More about Uriah and his work can be found at www.uriahbell.com